551.21 LIN

Lindeen,
Anatomy

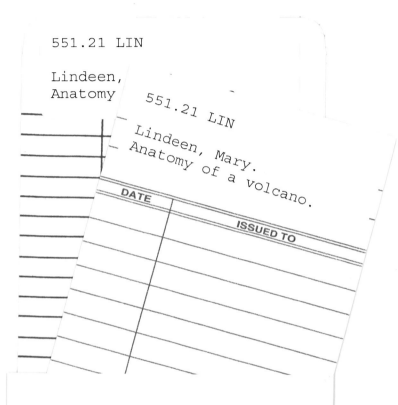

551.21 LIN

Lindeen, Mary.
Anatomy of a volcano.

DATE	ISSUED TO

Anatomy of a Volcano

Library of Congress Cataloging-in-Publication Data

Lindeen, Mary.
  Anatomy of a volcano / by Mary Lindeen.
      p. cm. -- (Shockwave)
  Includes index.
  ISBN-10: 0-531-17791-2 (lib. bdg.)
  ISBN-13: 978-0-531-17791-4 (lib. bdg.)
  ISBN-10: 0-531-15480-7 (pbk.)
  ISBN-13: 978-0-531-15480-9 (pbk.)

  1. Volcanoes--Juvenile literature. I. Title. II. Series.

  QE521.3.L55 2007
  551.21--dc22

2007007238

Published in 2008 by Children's Press, an imprint of Scholastic Inc.,
557 Broadway, New York, New York 10012
www.scholastic.com

09 10 11 12 13 14 15 16 17
10 9 8 7 6 5 4 3 2

Printed in China through Colorcraft Ltd., Hong Kong

Author: Mary Lindeen
Educational Consultant: Ian Morrison
Editor: Mary Atkinson
Designer: Anne Luo
Photo Researcher: Jamshed Mistry
Illustrations by: Anne Luo (pp. 8–9, 13)

Photographs by: Getty Images (p. 3; p. 7; p. 18; volcanologist and lava flow, pp. 22–23;
people and lahar flow, p. 27; Dante II robot, pp. 32–33); **Jennifer and Brian Lupton**
(teenagers, pp. 32–33); **Mary Atkinson** (Rangitoto Island, p. 30); **Photolibrary** (cover;
people cleaning up ashes, p. 11); **Tranz/Corbis** (damaged car, p. 11; p. 14; lava flow,
black-sand beach, p. 15; p. 17; pp. 19–21; volcanologists collecting lava and soil
samples, p. 23; pp. 24–25; Mount Pinatubo eruption, pp. 26–27; pp. 28–29; fern,
Kilauea, p. 30; p. 31)

All illustrations and other photographs © Weldon Owen Education Inc.

SHOCKWAVE
SCIENCE

Anatomy of a Volcano

Mary Lindeen

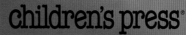

children's press®

An imprint of Scholastic Inc.

NEW YORK • TORONTO • LONDON • AUCKLAND • SYDNEY
MEXICO CITY • NEW DELHI • HONG KONG
DANBURY, CONNECTICUT

CHECK THESE OUT!

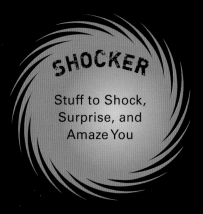

SHOCKER

Stuff to Shock,
Surprise, and
Amaze You

Quick Recaps
and Notable
Notes

Word Stunners
and Other Oddities

The Heads-Up
on Expert Reading

Links to More
Information

CONTENTS

HIGH-POWERED WORDS   6

GET ON THE WAVELENGTH   8

Instant Destruction   10

Red-Hot Rock   12

Fountains of Fire   14

Active, Asleep, or Dead?   16

Growing Mountains   18

The Gods Are Angry!   20

A High-Risk Job   22

The Biggest Bang of All   24

From Dormant to Deadly   26

A Steaming, Bubbling Powerhouse   28

Out of Death Comes Life   30

AFTERSHOCKS   32

GLOSSARY   34

FIND OUT MORE   35

INDEX   36

ABOUT THE AUTHOR   36

crater a large hole at the top of a volcano, which is left behind when lava, ash, and other material erupt out of the ground

dormant not erupting now, but has erupted in the past and may erupt again in the future

eruption the bursting out of the ground of lava, rock, gases, or ash onto the earth's surface or into the air

geothermal (*gee o THER muhl*) to do with the heat inside the earth

lava (*LA vuh*) melted rock that has come out of a volcano

magma melted rock that is inside the earth

pyroclastic flow (*pi ro KLAS tic FLO*) a fast-moving mass of very hot ash, gases, and bits of rock that rolls out of some volcanoes and along the ground

volcanologist a scientist who studies volcanoes

For additional vocabulary, see Glossary on page 34.

The prefix *pyro-* comes from the Greek word for fire, *pyros*. It is found at the beginning of quite a few words. For example, *pyrotechnics* is the craft of making and controlling firework displays. A *pyromaniac* is a person who has an irresistible urge to start fires.

An exploding volcano can rip apart a mountain in seconds. For humans and other living things, it is one of the most deadly natural disasters. Our only hope of surviving a violent **eruption** is to get away before it happens. From a safe distance, a volcano is an impressive site. Fountains of bright red **lava** spew out of the **crater**. Searing-hot clouds of gases and ash roar downhill. They often reach 100 miles per hour. Then, when the eruption is over, the landscape is changed forever.

People have always been fascinated by volcanoes. Today, scientists study them. We now know a great deal about what causes volcanoes. We know what happens when volcanoes erupt. The more we know, the more fascinating they become.

Instant Destruction

Imagine an explosion so strong that it rips 1,300 feet off a mountain in 30 seconds. Imagine an eruption so huge that about 10 million trees are flattened. That was what happened in the state of Washington when Mount St. Helens exploded.

Geologists had known that the eruption was coming. Earthquakes and much smaller eruptions had been happening for a few months. The mountain had started to bulge. Scientists knew that boiling-hot **magma** was building up underground. Then, at 8:32 A.M. on May 18, 1980, it happened: An earthquake triggered a huge explosion. This was followed by an **avalanche**. Then there was a blast of wind filled with ash and lava. It was a **pyroclastic flow**. People as far away as California and Idaho heard the explosion as the flow struck nearby Spirit Lake.

When the author says "Imagine an ...," I don't think she wants me to stop reading and start daydreaming! I think this is her way of getting my attention. It sure works for me!

The owner of this car parked it under some trees. He had no idea that the whole forest, as well as his car, would soon be destroyed.

Winds carried the ash east for about 930 miles. People covered their faces to protect their lungs as they cleaned up.

11

Red-Hot Rock

Many scientists believe that Earth has an inner core of solid metal. Around this is an outer core of melted metal. On top of that is a layer of extremely hot rock called the mantle. In much of the mantle, high pressure stops the rock from melting. However, pockets of melted rock form in some places. This melted rock is called magma.

Magma is lighter than the surrounding rock in the mantle. This causes it to rise upward. When it finds a weak place in Earth's rocky outer crust, it pushes through. This creates a volcano. The hot magma that flows – or explodes – out of the volcano is called lava.

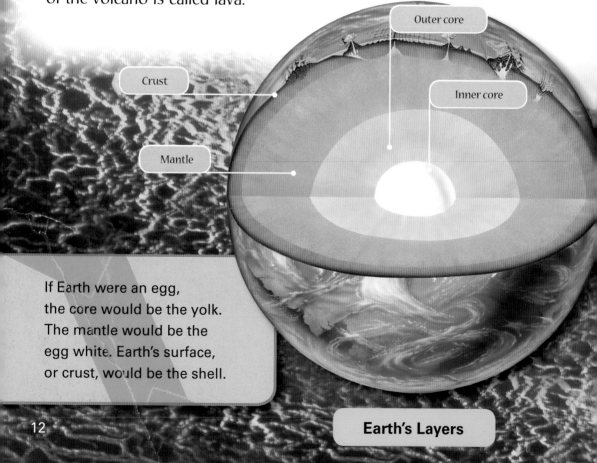

Outer core

Crust

Inner core

Mantle

If Earth were an egg, the core would be the yolk. The mantle would be the egg white. Earth's surface, or crust, would be the shell.

Earth's Layers

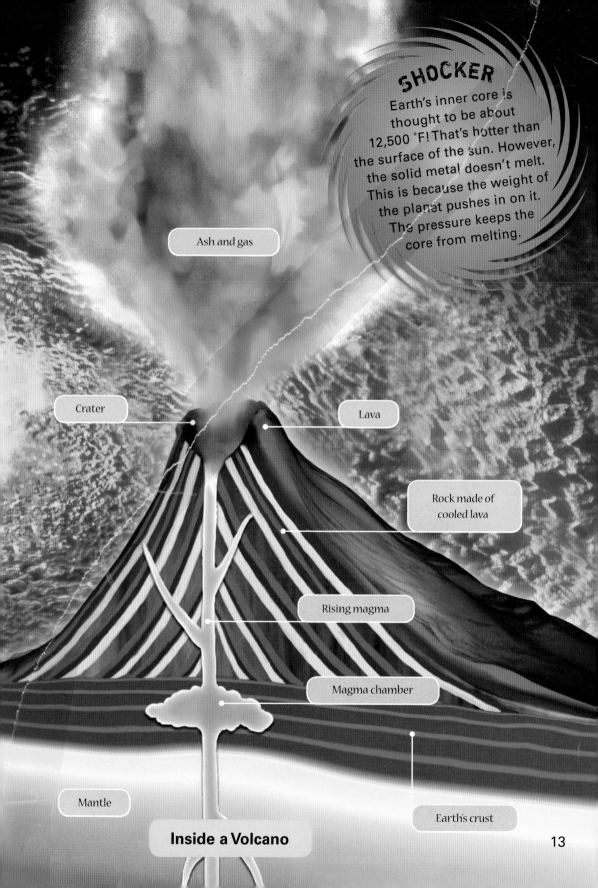

Ash and gas

Crater

Lava

Rock made of cooled lava

Rising magma

Magma chamber

Mantle

Earth's crust

Inside a Volcano

Fountains of Fire

Sometimes a spray of lava bursts out the top of a volcano. These fire fountains can reach hundreds of feet into the sky. Lumps of lava often cool into solid rock as they fly through the air. Rounded chunks are called bombs. Pieces with corners and sharp edges are called blocks. Both bombs and blocks can cause a great deal of damage.

At other times, lava flows smoothly out of a volcano. It oozes out the top and rolls slowly down the sides. As it cools, it hardens into layers of rock. Some lavas are runny and fast-flowing. They cool to form smooth rock. Other lavas are thick and sticky. They cool into hard, pointed chunks. The layers of lava often build up on top of each other, forming a volcanic mountain.

Volcanic Rocks
- Bombs: round chunks
- Blocks: lumps with corners and sharp edges
- Pumice: cooled lava with gas bubbles
- Obsidian: volcanic glass

Some lava is filled with bubbles of gas. It cools into rough, hole-filled rocks, such as pumice.

Lava that cools very quickly forms smooth volcanic glass, such as obsidian.

When flowing lava hits cool seawater, it shatters into tiny grains. These grains cool into black sand. There are black-sand beaches in volcanic places, such as Hawaii and Iceland.

15

Active, Asleep, or Dead?

Active volcanoes are volcanoes that are erupting right now. There are more than 1,000 active volcanoes in the world. They are found on every **continent**, except Australia. There are even active volcanoes in Antarctica and on the ocean floor. More than half of these active volcanoes are around the edge of the Pacific Ocean. This circle of volcanoes is called the Ring of Fire.

A **dormant** volcano is one that is quiet at the moment. It has erupted before and may erupt again. However, there may be years or even centuries between the eruptions. A volcano that is not expected to erupt again is called a dead, or extinct, volcano.

The Ring of Fire

ASIA

Japan

Philippines

Indonesia

INDIAN OCEAN

AUSTRALIA

New Zealand

PACIFIC OCEAN

NORTH AMERICA

SOUTH AMERICA

The crater of a dormant or an extinct volcano can fill with water. This creates a lake. Some, such as Crater Lake, are vacation spots. Others are filled with volcanic gases. The gases turn the water into hot, deadly acid.

Crater Lake, Oregon

SHOCKER
There are even volcanoes in space! The moon and some planets, such as Mars, have extinct volcanoes. There is evidence of active volcanoes on Venus.

One active volcano in southern Japan often produces clouds of ash and **debris**. Students living nearby must wear hard hats to and from school.

Growing Mountains

Tall volcanic mountains are often created in layers. Sometimes lava erupts and runs down the sides of a volcano. The lava cools and hardens into rock. At other times, there is a massive pyroclastic flow. The debris adds a new layer to the volcano, increasing its height. This kind of volcano is called a stratovolcano.

Mount Shasta is in California. It is one of many stratovolcanoes in the Pacific Northwest. It is 14,162 feet high.

Reading got much easier when I realized that each paragraph was about a different kind of volcano. That helped me understand some of the similarities and differences. The photos helped too!

Mauna Loa is in Hawaii.
It is a shield volcano.
Rivers of red-hot lava
flow down its sides.

Another kind of volcano is
called a shield volcano. A shield volcano is wide and not very
high. It erupts more quietly. Hot rivers of runny lava flow out
of cracks in the mountainside. As the lava hardens, it makes
the volcano wider and wider.

Cinder cones can build up in a single eruption. Clouds of ash
and bits of lava puff into the air. They fall to the ground, creating
a cone with a crater in the middle. Cinder cones often form
in groups. Sometimes they form
on top of other volcanoes.

Mauna Kea is also in Hawaii. It is an old
volcano with many cinder cones on its top.

The Gods Are Angry!

In the past, people did not know why volcanoes erupted. Some people thought they were a sign that the gods were angry. They made up stories to help them explain what was happening. Hawaiians said that the goddess Pele lived in Kilauea volcano. When she got mad, she made the volcano erupt.

The word *volcano* comes from the name of the Roman god of fire. The ancient Romans believed that Vulcan was a god who lived underground. He was a **blacksmith** who made tools for other gods. They thought that erupting mountains were Vulcan's chimneys. They named these mountains volcanoes.

Vulcan at His Forge by Peter Paul Rubens (1577–1640)

Many cities and states have a special name for their people. For example, Romans come from Rome; Parisians come from Paris; and Texans come from the state of Texas.

Today, some Hawaiians still honor ancient rituals, such as offering flowers to Pele.

In Japan, there is a folktale about Mount Fuji. In the story, a woman tells her husband that she is a goddess. She tells him that she is returning to her palace in the mountain. Then she gives him a magic mirror to see her image once she is gone. Her husband follows her, but he cannot find her. Unable to bear his grief, he jumps into the volcano. His love makes the mirror catch fire. The fire makes smoke come out of the mountain.

Mount Fuji

A High-Risk Job

Even modern science cannot **predict** exactly when a volcano will erupt. It is also impossible to prevent or stop an eruption. However, we now know more about volcanoes than ever before. This is thanks to the work of daring scientists called **volcanologists**. Volcanologists are volcano experts. They **monitor** volcanoes closely.

A volcanologist's suit blocks out the heat. But it also blocks a person's ability to easily see, hear, and move. These things can make it harder to work safely. They also make it harder to escape from sudden danger.

Volcanologists measure temperature changes in and around volcanoes. They use special **heat-resistant** equipment. Often they collect lava samples to study in a **laboratory**. They look for clues that will help us better understand volcanoes.

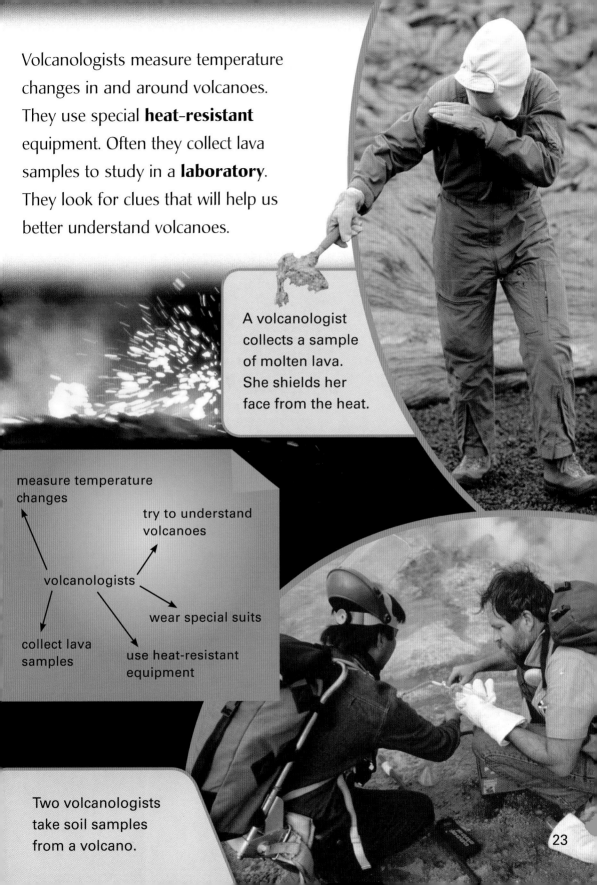

A volcanologist collects a sample of molten lava. She shields her face from the heat.

measure temperature changes

try to understand volcanoes

volcanologists

wear special suits

collect lava samples

use heat-resistant equipment

Two volcanologists take soil samples from a volcano.

The Biggest Bang of All

Volcanoes sometimes cause other deadly disasters. Large eruptions can trigger **tsunamis** and avalanches. They also affect the weather. They can create colder winters, heavy rains, and strong winds.

In 1883, Krakatau volcano in Indonesia erupted in a series of huge explosions. One explosion is thought to have been the loudest noise in history. It broke the eardrums of sailors up to 25 miles away. It was even heard by people in Australia, 2,000 miles away!

The explosions on Krakatau blew the 6,000-foot mountain to pieces. Old illustrations show us what it looked like before the eruption.

The explosions created 18 huge tsunamis. The tsunamis killed far more people than the actual eruptions. In all, more than 36,000 people died. Clouds of ash from the volcano blocked the sun. Far away, in Europe and the U.S., the temperatures were lower than usual for five years.

The largest tsunamis from Krakatau reached about 100 feet high.

Anak Krakatau is a new volcano. It is growing in the sea where part of Krakatau once stood. It erupts regularly.

From Dormant to Deadly

In 1991, Mount Pinatubo in the Philippines erupted. It killed more than 400 people. The volcano had been dormant for 600 years. Then it started blasting huge clouds of ash into the air.

Swirling, floating ash darkened the sky for days. A thick layer of ash covered everything for miles around. The people living near Mount Pinatubo could not breathe fresh air. Ash stung their eyes. It harmed their lungs.

Then it started to rain. It rained and rained. The rain turned the ash into mud. Rivers of mud, called **lahars**, rushed down the mountain. They destroyed whole villages. Many people died. Thousands more lost their homes.

A truck races away from the cloud of ash as Mount Pinatubo erupts.

The lahars on Mount Pinatubo continued long after the volcano stopped erupting. For the next few years, heavy rain often triggered a fresh lahar.

Mount Pinatubo:
- blasted ash into the air
- ash and rain combined as rivers of mud (lahars)
- lahars destroyed villages and homes

Lahar

27

A Steaming, Bubbling Powerhouse

Volcanoes are extremely dangerous, but they are also useful.
The heat from a volcano sometimes heats the water in the ground
nearby. When this hot water comes to the surface, it can create
hot springs or bubbling mud. For centuries, people have soaked
in hot springs and taken mud baths at these sites. Scientists have
figured out how to use this heat energy for other purposes.
It is used to heat buildings and create electricity.

In Japan, macaque monkeys live
on the slopes of Shirane volcano.
On cold days, they enjoy a soak
in the mountain's hot pools.

Gas from a volcano contains **sulfur**. It smells like rotten eggs. When the gas cools, the sulfur sometimes forms yellow crystals. Sulfur crystals are used for many things. For example, they are often used to strengthen rubber.

Kawah Ijen, Indonesia

In Iceland, hot water is pumped out of the ground and into pipes that heat homes. The country also has five main **geothermal** power plants. Steam from hot groundwater turns engines that create electricity.

The prefix *geo-* means "earth." The word *thermal* means "to do with heat." From this, we can figure out that the word *geothermal* has to do with heat from the earth.

The Blue Lagoon is a hot pool in Iceland. The hot water is pumped out of the ground. First it is used by a geothermal power plant. The engines at the plant are driven by steam from the hot water. The excess water then flows into the pool.

29

Out of Death Comes Life

A volcano can destroy a huge forest within just minutes or hours. But it will take hundreds of years before the bare rock becomes forest. Lichens, mosses, and ferns are usually the first to settle the new land. Their **spores** are blown onto the rock by the wind. Small flowering plants arrive next. Their roots help break up some of the hard volcanic rock. Tiny pieces of lava mix with dead

Scientists study the plants that grow at Kilauea in Hawaii. They have noticed that ferns often grow in the cracks in the lava.

plant matter to become rich, **fertile** soil. Eventually, trees can take root. The volcano's deadly path has led to new life.

Rangitoto Island is in New Zealand. About 600 years ago, it erupted out of the sea. Today, 200 different trees and flowering plants grow on the island. It is on its way to becoming mature forest.

Land that lies far enough away from a volcano to avoid damage often receives a light layer of ash. This volcanic ash is full of **nutrients**. It helps create some of the best farmland in the world. The risk of living near a volcano can pay off if you're lucky!

SHOCKER

A few visitors to Kilauea in Hawaii have died after sneaking into forbidden areas. The ground there is often unstable. It is much more dangerous than it looks.

Tungurahua volcano is in Ecuador. It regularly sends up clouds of ash. The ash falls over nearby farmland. As a result, the land is very fertile.

Volcanologists do important work. They help us understand volcanoes better. As a result, people living near a volcano can often **evacuate** the area before an eruption. This saves many lives. However, poisonous gases, flying lava, and unstable ground make volcanology dangerous. Where possible, volcanologists use robots and monitoring devices to do the work for them.

WHAT DO YOU THINK?

Would you be willing to risk your life for a job such as volcanology? Is it fair to the people who care about you?

PRO

I would risk my life if the job was worth it. It is good that some people risk their lives to save others. Without volcanologists, thousands or even millions more people might be killed by volcanoes.

Dante II (left) is a robotic volcanologist. It explored the crater of Mount Spurr in Alaska. However, it had problems moving over the uneven ground inside the crater.

CON

I wouldn't do it. My parents would worry too much. If I were a volcanologist, I would focus on developing better robots and other monitoring devices. That way, I could study volcanoes with much less risk.

GLOSSARY

avalanche (*A vuh lanch*) a large amount of rock, earth, or snow that falls down a mountain

blacksmith someone who makes things out of iron

continent one of the seven main land masses on Earth, such as North America and Asia

debris (*duh BREE*) lots of small pieces of rock

evacuate (*e VAK yu ate*) to leave a place because it is too dangerous

fertile (*FUR tuhl*) full of nutrients that help plants grow

geologist a scientist who studies the rock and soil layers that make up Earth

heat-resistant able to withstand very high temperatures

laboratory a room where scientists perform experiments and study their results

lahar (*la HAR*) a river of mud made up of volcanic ash and water

monitor to keep watch over something. It can involve taking regular measurements, such as temperature recordings.

nutrients substances that help living things to be healthy and grow

predict to say that a particular event will happen

spore a seed-like structure that grows into a new plant

sulfur (*SUHL fur*) a yellow chemical element found in the earth

tsunami (*tsu NAH mee*) an enormous wave caused by an earthquake or a volcano

Tsunami

FIND OUT MORE

BOOKS

Adams, Simon. *The Best Book of Volcanoes*. Kingfisher, 2001.

Caplan, Jeremy. *Volcanoes!* HarperCollins, 2006.

DK Publishing. *Volcano*. DK Children, 2006.

Lindeen, Mary. *Ashes to Ashes: Uncovering Pompeii*. Scholastic Inc., 2008.

Mallory, Kenneth. *Diving to a Deep-Sea Volcano*. Houghton Mifflin, 2006.

O'Meara, Donna. *Into the Volcano*. Kids Can Press, 2005.

Van Rose, Susanna. *Volcano & Earthquake*. DK Publishing, 2004.

WEB SITES

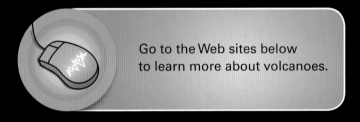

Go to the Web sites below
to learn more about volcanoes.

www.fema.gov/kids/volcano

www.nationalgeographic.com/ngkids/0312

http://volcano.und.nodak.edu

http://kids.discovery.com/games/pompeii/pompeii.html

INDEX

ash 8, 10–11, 13, 17, 19, 25–27, 31
California 10, 18
cinder cones 19
craters 8, 13, 17, 19, 33
Ecuador 31
geothermal power 29
Hawaii 15, 19–21, 30–31
hot springs 28–29
Iceland 15, 29
Japan 16–17, 21, 28
Krakatau 24–25
lahars 26–27
lava bombs 14–15
magma 10, 12–13
Mars 17
Mount Fuji 21

Mount Pinatubo 26–27
Mount St. Helens 10
New Zealand 16, 30
obsidian 15
Pele 20–21
Philippines 16, 26–27
pumice 15
pyroclastic flows 10, 18
Ring of Fire 16
shield volcanoes 19
space 17
stratovolcanoes 18
sulfur 29
tsunamis 24–25
volcanologists 22–23, 32–33
Vulcan 20

ABOUT THE AUTHOR

Mary Lindeen saw her first volcano when she visited Hawaii as a student teacher. She thought it might be boring – just black rocks and not much to look at. She was wrong! The volcanoes in Hawaii were beautiful, whether they were old extinct ones covered with lush, green vegetation, or active volcanoes that might spit out lava at any minute. When she had a chance to write about volcanoes, she erupted with delight!